ISLAND HERITAGE™
PUBLISHING
A DIVISION OF THE MADDEN CORPORATION

94-411 Kō'aki Street
Waipahu, Hawai'i 96797-2806
Orders: (800) 468-2800
Information: (808) 564-8800
Fax: (808) 564-8877
islandheritage.com

ISBN: 1-59700-506-1
First Edition, First Printing–2007

Photography by Ron Dahlquist
Text by Kirsten Whatley

ABOVE
MAUI

Moloka'i & Lāna'i

RON DAHLQUIST

The islet of Molokini lures divers and snorkelers to explore its underwater stage, where exotic fish and colorful coral entertain.

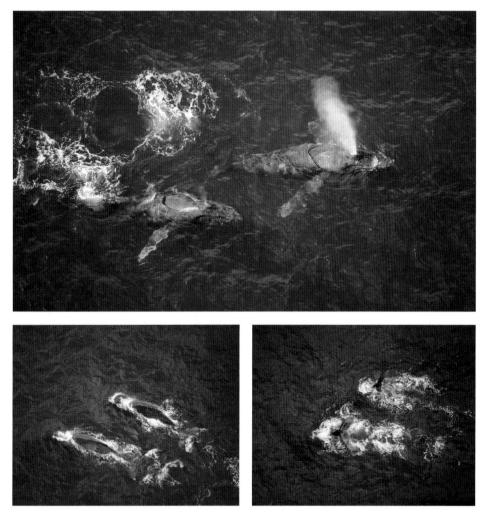

Up to eight thousand humpback whales make the marathon swim from Alaska to Hawai'i's breeding grounds each winter—nearly 75 percent can be found in Maui's waters, where they delight spectators with breathtaking displays.

Puʻu Ōlaʻi ("earthquake hill") separates Big Beach from its neighboring cove, Little Beach. The rugged cinder cone is said to have been one of Maui's last to erupt.

Commonly known as Big Beach, this arid coastline in Mākena stretches over three thousand feet against a *kiawe* forest backdrop.

Rocky Wailea Point gives way to sloping shoreline on either side, creating a swimmers' paradise. Its name means the "waters of Lea," goddess of canoe makers and the name of a fish deity said to stand watch over this point.

The Mākena South golf course, one of Maui's many greens with a view, curves along the hilly landscape.

Nested into Wailea's Gold and Emerald golf courses, a clubhouse and restaurant offer respite from the shimmering sun.

The Kāhili and King Kamehameha golf courses are carved into the region of Waikapū, which translates as "water of the conch." Legend has it that a conch shell used to sound continuously in this area and be audible throughout the islands.

Sixty acres of tropical trees and plants in central Maui make up the mosaic of Maui Tropical Plantation.

One of the island's windiest spots, the hills above Māʻalaea house a series of energy-generating windmills.

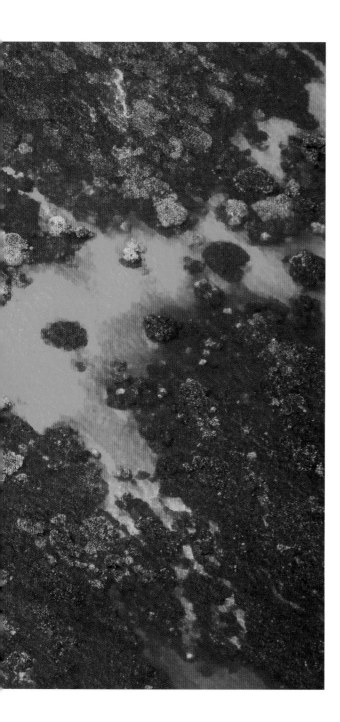

A fantastical coral garden off the shores of Olowalu invites kayakers and snorkelers to dip in for a closer look.

The view toward land reveals a sun-warmed coast with the West Maui Mountains beyond.

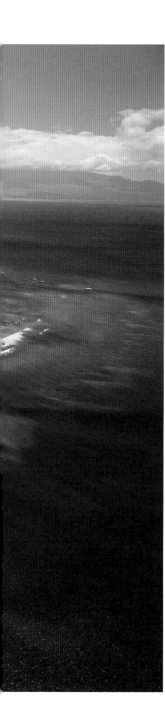

Olowalu's upland tapestry mirrors its offshore grandeur in hues of sea-foam green and cerulean blue.

In Olowalu's "many hills" (the literal meaning of its name), petroglyphs inscribed on steep rock faces tell the story of the area's people.

Lahaina is known for its colorful past as a whaling port, but in the times of kings, rows of taro stretched along its beachfront, while breadfruit trees provided shade.

The Kā'anapali resort complex spans three miles of blushing sand, with Black Rock at its center—the westernmost point of the island.

Kāʻanapali is a veritable playground, offering multiple luxury hotels, condominium complexes, water sports, golf courses, and cultural entertainment.

Black Rock, or Puʻu Kekaʻa ("the rumble"), has become a popular snorkelers' haven, while the adjacent shoreline serves the needs of sunbathers and swimmers.

The resort area of Kapalua provides idyllic views of Moloka'i across Pailolo Channel.

Embraced by two rocky points, Kapalua's tranquil beach is considered the west side's safest for swimming.

Craggy Hāwea Point separates the sands of Kapalua Beach on its right from Oneloa Beach on its left.

Honolua, the large bay on the right, was traditionally used for the community activity of netting *akule* fish. Today, it is a sea life sanctuary and a draw for snorkelers.

Farming and shore fishing denote the bulk of activity in Kahakuloa, on West Maui's isolated northern coast.

Pu'u Koa'e, on the right side of the bay, is the legendary site of Kahekili's Leap—a cliff-hanging spot several hundred feet above sea level, from where the eighteenth-century king would jump for his morning swim before climbing back up the mountain for breakfast.

A replica 1935 Waco biplane soars above Maui's rugged north coast.

Many of Maui's north shore beaches, such as Spreckelsville (at left), combine wind and wave power to provide prime windsurfing conditions.

Named for a prominent sugar refiner, Spreckelsville once boasted two schools, several plantation camps, and a host of seaside residences. The sands are popularly known as Baldwin Beach, and the reef-protected swath in the photo at left as Baby Beach.

Today, Spreckelsville is a wide stretch of windswept sands that run all the way to Kanahā in the west.

A former sugar plantation town, Pāʻia is now the gathering grounds for local artists, hippies, and the windsurfing elite. Host to at least a dozen eateries and chic boutiques, it often lives up to its name, which means "noisy."

Along the gradual rise of Haleakalā, sugarcane and pineapple fields turn the terrain into a living patchwork.

Upcountry meadows stay a vibrant shade of green due to the area's abundant rainfall—in the light of the tropic sun, this often means rainbows.

Auburn tufts of foliage dot Haleakalā's otherwise green-toned slopes.

The highway above Kula snakes its way up the mountain face toward Haleakalā's summit.

'Ulupalakua Ranch unfurls in acres of green—from six thousand feet in elevation all the way to the sea. Before sporting cattle, it was a sugar plantation and favored destination for Hawaiian royalty.

A stark and stunning moonscape, Haleakalā ("house of the sun") reigns at over ten thousand feet above sea level. The observatories (above right) are overseen by the University of Hawai'i Institute for Astronomy, and are collectively called Science City.

The sinuous road to Hāna makes at least six hundred turns and twists on its journey to the distant rural town.

As it wraps around the emerald folds, the highway affords ocean views that reach unhindered to the horizon.

A much-used boat ramp makes entry and exit from Māliko Bay accessible. Here, fishermen net the schooling *akule* and *'ōpelu* that populate its waters.

Honomanū Bay once supported a large community, with extensive *lo'i* (taro patches) growing on both sides of the valley's stream.

The Keʻanae peninsula's sweeping fan of lava stretches far into the ocean.

Since antiquity, the peninsula has been synonymous with taro cultivation, and is known for its *poi*, or pounded taro root, a traditional staple food.

The striking black sands of 120-acre Waiʻānapanapa State Park bear the name Paʻiloa, or "always splashing"—an apt description of their exposure to the rough open ocean.

Hāna town and its pockets of paradise make this jewel a well-earned destination of the infamous winding road.

Hāna and its environs are replete with ancient history—the region is said to be the home of Māui, the demigod; the birthplace of Queen Kaʻahumanu; and a legendary resting spot for Pele, goddess of volcanoes.

The largest *heiau* (ancient place of worship) in the islands, Pi'ilani Heiau outside of Hāna is believed to have been erected in the sixteenth century. It is now part of Kahanu Garden, a division of the larger National Tropical Botanical Garden.

Surrounded by thirty-foot sea cliffs, Hāmoa Beach is one of East Maui's many coastal gems.

Hidden pockets of emerald and turquoise adorn the island's curvaceous coastline.

At the end of a bamboo forest trail through Kīpahulu's ʻOheʻo Gulch, Waimoku Falls looms from impassable heights.

Another dramatic falls dampens Haleakalā's slopes.

The ʻOheʻo Pools attract throngs of visitors each day to this eastern appendage of Haleakalā National Park.

Heavy rains in the higher altitudes keep downslope streams and waterfalls in a continuous race toward the sea.

From above, lacy upper Wailua Falls is as eye-catching as when viewed from below.

The road connecting Kaupō with the more populated side of the island traverses dramatic and desolate scenery, and a string of changing climates.

On East Maui's southern shores, Hui Aloha church stands a lone sentinel in windswept Kaupō.

Protected since 1973, the ʻĀhihi-Kīnaʻu Natural Area Reserve makes the lava flows of the cape and inshore marine area a sanctuary for local wildlife.

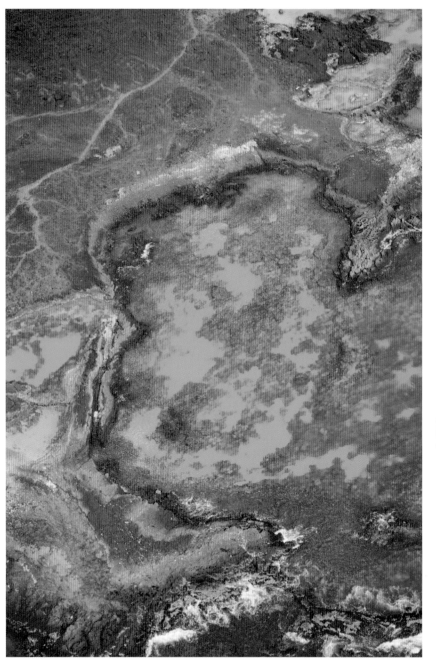

A closer view reveals the shocking hues and shapes of this unusual waterfront.

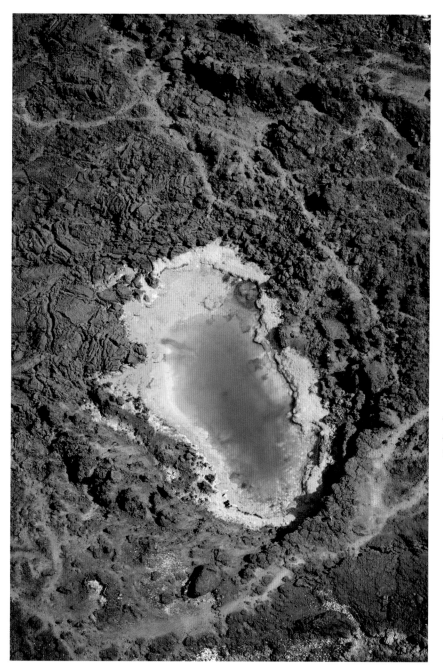

This rare anchialine pond is an example of the fragile ecosystem that survives within the reserve's lava.

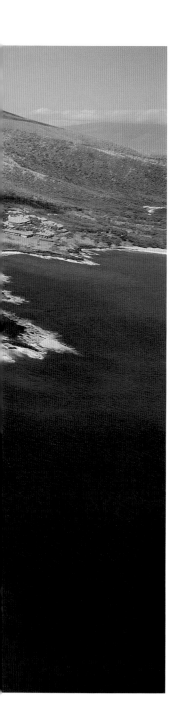

High atop the lava-ringed bluffs of Lānaʻi, the Challenge at Mānele—
designed by Jack Nicklaus—draws golfers seeking pure peace.

Pu'u Pehe, once part of Lāna'i's mainland, has separated into its own islet due to years of wave-inspired erosion. Commonly known as Sweetheart Rock, legend tells of a young Maui woman and a Lāna'i warrior whose lives fatefully ended here.

Off the eastern coast of Moloka'i, Mokuho'oniki islet became a bombing target during WWII and for many years to follow. Today, it is a protected bird refuge.

Moloka'i's north shore cliffs pierce the heavens
with near-vertical precision, forming a massive and
verdant seafront.

In Kalawao, the original site of the Hansen's disease colony on Molokaʻi's Kalaupapa peninsula, a congregational church formed just after the first patients arrived in 1866. Its members named it Siloama, Church of the Healing Spring.